About the Author

Saul E. Sanchez is a seasoned data scientist and software engineer with a passion for leveraging data to drive innovation. With a strong foundation in statistical modeling, machine learning, and programming languages like Python, Saul Sanchez has a proven track record of delivering impactful data-driven solutions.

Saul Sanchez excels in data analysis, feature engineering, model building, and deployment. Their expertise spans a wide range of techniques, including supervised and unsupervised learning, deep learning, and natural language processing. They are proficient in using tools like TensorFlow, PyTorch, Scikit-learn, and Pandas to extract valuable insights from complex datasets.

Beyond technical skills, Saul Sanchez is dedicated to ethical AI and data privacy. They strive to develop models that are fair, transparent, and responsible.

TABLE OF CONTENTS

PART I: INTRODUCTION TO CLOUD COMPUTING

CHAPTER 1: UNDERSTANDING CLOUD COMPUTING
WHAT IS CLOUD COMPUTING
KEYS CHARACTERISTICS OF CLOUD COMPUTING
TYPES OF CLOUD DEPLOYMENT MODELS
BENEFITS AND CHALLENGES OF CLOUD COMPUTING

CHAPTER 2: ORACLE CLOUD INFRASTRUCTURE (OCI) OVERVIEW
INTRODUCTION TO OCI
CORE SERVICES OF OCI
COMPUTE SERVICES (Virtual Machines, Bare Metal Instances)
STORAGE SERVICES (Block Storage, Object Storage, File Storage)
NETWORKING SERVICES (Virtual Cloud Networks, Load Balancing, Security Lists)
DATABASE SERVICES (Autonomous Database, Database Cloud)

PART II: IMPLEMENTING CLOUD-BASED IT SOLUTIONS

CHAPTER 3: PLANNING AND DESIGNING CLOUD SOLUTIONS
IDENTIFYING CLOUD-SUITABLE WORKLOADS
ASSESSING CLOUD READINESS
DESIGNING CLOUD ARCHITECTURES
SECURITY CONSIDERATIONS IN CLOUD ENVIRONMENTS

CHAPTER 4: MIGRATING TO THE CLOUD
MIGRATION STRATEGIES (Lift-and-Shift, Re-Platforming, Re-Architecting)
MIGRATION TOOLS AND TECHNIQUES
CHALLENGES AND BEST PRACTICES FOR CLOUD MIGRATION

CHAPTER 5: MANAGING AND OPERATING CLOUD ENVIRONMENTS
OCI CONSOLE AND CLI
RESOURCE MANAGEMENT AND COST OPTIMIZATION
MONITORING AND LOGGING
AUTOMATION AND SCRIPTING (Terraform, Ansible)
DISASTER RECOVERY AND BUSINESS CONTINUITY

PART III: ADVANCED TOPICS IN ORACLE CLOUD

CHAPTER 6: SECURITY IN THE CLOUD
IDENTITY AND ACCESS MANAGEMENT (IAM)
NETWORK SECURITY (Firewalls, Security Lists, VPNs)
DATA SECURITY AND ENCRYPTION
THREAT DETECTION AND RESPONSE

PRACTICAL ORACLE CLOUD COMPUTING

Implementing Cloud-Based IT Solutions

Saul E Sanchez

Copyright © 2024 by Saul E.Sanchez. All rights reserved.

No part of this book may be reproduced in any form or by any electronic or mechanical means, including information storage and retrieval systems, without permission in writing from the publisher, except by a reviewer who may quote brief passages in a review.

This book and parts thereof may not be reproduced in any form, stored in a retrieval system, or transmitted in any form by any means—electronic, mechanical, photocopy, recording, or otherwise—without prior written permission of the publisher, except as provided by United States of America copyright law.

Disclaimer

The information contained within this book is intended for general knowledge and informational purposes only. It is not a substitute for professional advice. While all efforts have been made to ensure accuracy, the author(s) and publisher cannot guarantee the completeness or accuracy of the information presented.

The author(s) and publisher assume no responsibility for any errors, omissions, or damages arising from the use of the information contained herein. Readers are encouraged to verify information with additional sources and consult with professionals as needed.

The inclusion of any third-party content or links does not constitute an endorsement or recommendation by the author(s) or publisher.

CHAPTER 7: DATABASE AND ANALYTICS
AUTONOMOUS DATABASE
DATA WAREHOUSE CLOUD
ANALYTICS CLOUD
MACHINE LEARNING AND AI SERVICES

CHAPTER 8: SERVERLESS COMPUTING
FUNCTIONS AS A SERVICE (FAAS)
CONTAINER-BASED SERVICES

CHAPTER 9: INTEGRATION AND API MANAGEMENT
INTEGRATION CLOUD
API PLATFORM CLOUD

PART IV: REAL-WORLD USE CASES AND BEST PRACTICES

CHAPTER 10: CASE STUDY: MIGRATING A TRADITIONAL DATA CENTER TO OCI
CHALLENGES AND CONSIDERATIONS
MIGRATION STEPS AND BEST PRACTICES
LESSONS LEARNED

CHAPTER 11: BUILDING A SCALABLE WEB APPLICATION ON OCI
ARCHITECTURE DESIGN
DEPLOYMENT AND CONFIGURATION
PERFORMANCE OPTIMIZATION AND MONITORING

CHAPTER 12: IMPLEMENTING A DATA LAKE AND DATA WAREHOUSE ON OCI
DATA INGESTION AND TRANSFORMATION
DATA ANALYSIS AND VISUALIZATION
DATA SECURITY AND GOVERNANCE

APPENDIX A: OCI CERTIFICATIONS
APPENDIX B: GLOSSARY OF CLOUD TERMS

PART I: INTRODUCTION TO CLOUD COMPUTING

CHAPTER 1: UNDERSTANDING CLOUD COMPUTING

WHAT IS CLOUD COMPUTING

Cloud computing is a transformative technology that has revolutionized the way businesses and individuals consume IT resources. It involves delivering computing services—such as servers, storage, databases, networking, software, analytics, and intelligence—over the Internet ("the cloud"). Instead of owning and maintaining physical data centers and servers, users access these resources on an as-needed basis from cloud service providers.

Key Characteristics of Cloud Computing:

1. On-Demand Self-Service: Users can access cloud resources independently, without requiring significant human interaction with a service provider.

2. Broad Network Access: Cloud services are accessible via a variety of devices, including computers, smartphones, and tablets, through a network connection.

3. Resource Pooling: Cloud providers pool physical resources to serve multiple consumers using a multi-tenant model.

4. Rapid Elasticity: Resources can be rapidly provisioned and released, allowing organizations to scale up or down based on demand.

5. Measured Service: Cloud services are often billed based on usage, providing a pay-as-you-go model.

Benefits of Cloud Computing:

- Cost-Effectiveness: Reduced upfront costs, pay-as-you-go pricing, and economies of scale.

- Scalability: Easily scale resources up or down to meet changing demands.

- Flexibility: Access resources from anywhere with an internet connection.

- Reliability: Cloud providers invest heavily in redundancy and disaster recovery.

- Security: Robust security measures to protect data and applications.

- Innovation: Focus on core business activities while leveraging cutting-edge cloud technologies.

Cloud computing offers a flexible, scalable, and cost-effective way to deliver IT services, empowering organizations to innovate faster and achieve greater agility.

KEYS CHARACTERISTICS OF CLOUD COMPUTING

Cloud computing is characterized by several key features that differentiate it from traditional IT infrastructure:

1. On-Demand Self-Service:
- Users can independently provision cloud resources without requiring significant human interaction with a service provider.
- This empowers users to quickly spin up virtual machines, storage volumes, and other resources as needed.
- Self-service portals and APIs enable users to manage their cloud environments with ease.

2. Broad Network Access:
- Cloud services are accessible via a variety of devices, including computers, smartphones, and tablets, through a network connection.
- This flexibility allows users to work from anywhere with an internet connection, promoting remote work and collaboration.

3. Resource Pooling:
- Cloud providers pool physical resources to serve multiple consumers using a multi-tenant model.
- This allows for efficient resource utilization and cost savings, as multiple users share the same underlying infrastructure.
- Cloud providers manage the allocation and scaling of resources to ensure optimal performance and availability.

4. Rapid Elasticity:
- Cloud resources can be rapidly provisioned and released, allowing organizations to scale up or down based on demand.
- This enables organizations to quickly respond to fluctuations in workload, such as seasonal peaks or unexpected surges in traffic.
- By avoiding overprovisioning, organizations can optimize resource utilization and reduce costs.

5. Measured Service:
- Cloud services are often billed based on usage, providing a pay-as-you-go model.
- This eliminates the need for significant upfront investments in hardware and software.
- Organizations can pay only for the resources they consume, optimizing costs and aligning IT expenses with business needs.

TYPES OF CLOUD DEPLOYMENT MODELS

Cloud computing offers various deployment models to cater to different organizational needs and risk tolerances. Here are the primary types:

1. Public Cloud:

A public cloud is a cloud computing environment offered by a third-party service provider. It is accessible to the general public over the internet. Public cloud providers manage the infrastructure, security, and maintenance of the cloud environment.

Key Characteristics:

- Shared Resources: Multiple organizations share the same physical infrastructure.
- Pay-as-You-Go Pricing: Users pay only for the resources they consume.
- High Scalability: Resources can be quickly scaled up or down to meet changing demands.
- Rapid Deployment:** New applications and services can be deployed quickly.

Examples: Amazon Web Services (AWS), Microsoft Azure, Google Cloud Platform (GCP)

2. Private Cloud:

A private cloud is a cloud computing environment dedicated to a single organization. It can be hosted on-premises or off-premises, but it is exclusively for the organization's use. Private clouds offer greater control and security but can be more expensive to set up and maintain.

Key Characteristics:

- Dedicated Resources: The organization has exclusive access to the resources.
- High Security: Enhanced security measures can be implemented to protect sensitive data.
- Customization: The cloud environment can be tailored to specific organizational needs.
- Complex Management: Requires significant IT expertise to manage and maintain.

3. Hybrid Cloud:

A hybrid cloud combines the benefits of both public and private clouds. It involves deploying applications and data across multiple cloud environments, allowing organizations to leverage the best of both worlds. Hybrid clouds provide flexibility, scalability, and cost-effectiveness, while also addressing data security and compliance concerns.

Key Characteristics:
- Data Portability: Data can be easily moved between public and private clouds.
- Enhanced Security: Sensitive data can be stored in a private cloud while non-sensitive data can be stored in a public cloud.
- Disaster Recovery: Hybrid clouds can be used for disaster recovery and business continuity.

- Complex Management: Requires careful planning and orchestration to manage multiple cloud environments.

4. Multi-Cloud:

A multi-cloud strategy involves utilizing multiple cloud providers to deploy applications and data. This approach can help organizations avoid vendor lock-in, improve performance, and enhance disaster recovery capabilities. However, managing multiple cloud environments can be complex and requires careful planning and orchestration.

Key Characteristics:

- Vendor Diversity: Reduces reliance on a single cloud provider.
- Optimized Performance: Applications can be deployed on the most suitable cloud platform.
- Disaster Recovery: Multiple cloud providers can be used for redundancy and failover.
- Increased Complexity: Managing multiple cloud environments requires advanced skills and tools.

By understanding these deployment models, organizations can choose the best approach to meet their specific needs and achieve their business objectives.

BENEFITS AND CHALLENGES OF CLOUD COMPUTING

Cost-Effectiveness:

- Reduced upfront costs for hardware and software.

- Pay-as-you-go pricing model, allowing organizations to pay only for the resources they consume.

- Economies of scale, as cloud providers can leverage shared infrastructure to offer competitive pricing.

Scalability:

- Rapidly scale resources up or down to meet fluctuating demands.

- Easily accommodate growth and seasonal variations.

- Avoid overprovisioning and underutilization of resources.

Flexibility:

- Access resources from anywhere with an internet connection.
- Enable remote work and collaboration.
- Support a variety of devices and operating systems.

Reliability:

- Robust infrastructure with built-in redundancy and fault tolerance.
- High availability and disaster recovery capabilities.
- Reduced downtime and improved business continuity.

Security:

- Advanced security measures to protect data and applications.
- Regular security updates and patches.
- Expert security teams to monitor and respond to threats.

Innovation:

- Focus on core business activities by offloading IT infrastructure management.
- Access to cutting-edge technologies and services.
- Faster time to market for new products and services.

CHALLENGES OF CLOUD COMPUTING

Vendor Lock-in:

- Reliance on a specific cloud provider can make it difficult to migrate to another provider.
- Potential for increased costs and reduced flexibility.

Security Concerns:

- Sharing infrastructure with other organizations can increase the risk of security breaches.
- Data privacy and compliance concerns may arise.

Network Dependency:

- Reliance on a stable internet connection.
- Potential performance issues due to network latency or bandwidth limitations.

Skill Gap:

- Requires specialized skills to manage and optimize cloud environments.
- Need for training and upskilling of IT professionals.

Cost Management:

- Potential for unexpected costs if not managed carefully.
- Need for robust cost monitoring and optimization strategies.

By understanding both the benefits and challenges, organizations can effectively leverage cloud computing to achieve their business goals while mitigating risks.

CHAPTER 2: ORACLE CLOUD INFRASTRUCTURE (OCI) OVERVIEW

INTRODUCTION TO OCI

Oracle Cloud Infrastructure (OCI) is a comprehensive cloud computing platform offered by Oracle. It provides a wide range of services, including compute, storage, networking, database, analytics, and artificial intelligence, enabling organizations to build, deploy, and manage applications in a scalable and secure manner.

Key Features of OCI:

- High Performance: OCI offers high-performance computing instances, including bare metal servers and GPU-accelerated instances, to handle demanding workloads.

- Advanced Security: Robust security features, such as encryption, identity and access management, and network security, protect sensitive data and applications.

- Global Infrastructure: A vast global network of data centers allows organizations to deploy applications and data closer to their users, reducing latency and improving performance.

- Integration with Oracle Software: Seamless integration with Oracle's enterprise software, such as Oracle Database, Oracle Middleware, and Oracle Applications.

- Serverless Computing: Offers Functions as a Service (FaaS) and Container Engine for Kubernetes (OKE) to build and deploy serverless applications.

- Data Science and Machine Learning: Provides a comprehensive suite of tools and services for data science, machine learning, and artificial intelligence.

Benefits of Using OCI:

- Scalability: Easily scale resources up or down to meet changing demands.

- Cost-Effectiveness: Pay-as-you-go pricing model and optimized resource utilization.

- Performance: High-performance computing instances and advanced networking capabilities.

- Security: Robust security features to protect sensitive data.

- Global Reach: Deploy applications and data across multiple regions.

- Integration with Oracle Software: Seamless integration with Oracle's enterprise software.
Innovation: Access to cutting-edge technologies and services.

CORE SERVICES OF OCI

OCI offers a comprehensive suite of cloud services to cater to diverse organizational needs. Some of the core services include:

1. Compute Services:

- Virtual Machines (VMs): Flexible compute instances that can be customized to meet specific workload requirements.
- Bare Metal Instances: High-performance physical servers for demanding workloads.
- Compute Instances: A variety of instance shapes and sizes to accommodate different workloads.

2. Storage Services:

- Block Storage: High-performance, low-latency block storage volumes for critical applications.
- Object Storage: Durable and scalable object storage for storing large amounts of data.
- File Storage: Shared file systems for easy access to data across multiple instances.

3. Networking Services:

- Virtual Cloud Networks (VCNs): Customizable virtual networks to isolate and secure workloads.
- Load Balancing: Distributes traffic across multiple instances to improve performance and reliability.
- Security Lists: Network security rules to control inbound and outbound traffic.

4. Database Services:

- Autonomous Database: Fully managed database service that automates database tasks, such as patching, backups, and tuning.
- Database Cloud: A fully managed database service that provides a variety of database options, including Oracle Database, MySQL, and PostgreSQL.

These core services provide the building blocks for a wide range of cloud-based applications and solutions. By combining these services, organizations can create highly scalable, reliable, and secure cloud environments.

COMPUTE SERVICES (Virtual Machines, Bare Metal Instances)

OCI offers a variety of compute services to meet diverse workload requirements. Two of the primary compute services are:

1. Virtual Machines (VMs):

Virtual Machines (VMs) are virtualized computing environments that simulate physical servers. They provide flexible and scalable compute resources, allowing organizations to deploy and manage applications in a virtualized environment.

Key Features:

- Customization: VMs can be customized with different operating systems, software, and configurations.
- Scalability: Easily scale VMs up or down to meet changing workloads.
- Cost-Effective: Pay only for the resources consumed.
- Isolation: VMs are isolated from each other, providing enhanced security.

2. Bare Metal Instances:

Bare Metal Instances provide direct access to physical server hardware. They offer high performance and low latency, making them ideal for demanding workloads such as high-performance computing, data analytics, and machine learning.

Key Features:

- High Performance: Direct access to physical hardware for optimal performance.
- Flexibility: Customize the hardware configuration to meet specific needs.
- Security: Enhanced security features to protect sensitive data.
- Complex Management: Requires more advanced management skills compared to VMs.

By understanding the differences between VMs and Bare Metal Instances, organizations can choose the right compute service for their specific workload requirements.

STORAGE SERVICES (Block Storage, Object Storage, File Storage)

OCI offers a range of storage services to meet various data storage needs:

1. Block Storage:

Block Storage provides raw block storage volumes that can be attached to compute instances. It is ideal for applications that require high performance and low latency, such as databases and high-performance computing workloads.

Key Features:

- High Performance: Low-latency access to data.
- Flexibility: Create and delete volumes as needed.
- Scalability: Easily increase or decrease storage capacity.

2. Object Storage:

Object Storage is a scalable and durable storage service for storing large amounts of unstructured data. It is suitable for storing data such as images, videos, logs, and backups.

Key Features:

- Scalability: Automatically scales to store virtually unlimited amounts of data.
- Durability: Data is replicated across multiple availability domains for redundancy.
- Cost-Effective: Pay only for the storage used.

3. File Storage:

File Storage provides shared file systems that can be accessed by multiple compute instances. It is ideal for sharing data between applications and users.

Key Features:

- Shared Access: Multiple instances can access the same file system.
- Scalability: Easily scale storage capacity to meet growing needs.
- Performance: High-performance file system for demanding workloads.

By understanding the differences between these storage services, organizations can choose the right storage solution for their specific data storage needs.

NETWORKING SERVICES (Virtual Cloud Networks, Load Balancing, Security Lists)

OCI provides a comprehensive set of networking services to build secure and scalable network environments.

1. Virtual Cloud Networks (VCNs):

VCNs are software-defined networks that allow you to isolate your resources and control traffic flow. You can create subnets within a VCN to segment your network and apply security policies to specific groups of resources.

Key Features:

- Isolation: Segment your network into subnets to control traffic flow.
- Security: Implement security rules to protect your network from unauthorized access.
- Scalability: Easily scale your network to meet growing demands.

2. Load Balancing:

Load Balancing distributes incoming traffic across multiple instances to improve performance and reliability. OCI offers both Layer 4 and Layer 7 load balancing.

Key Features:

- High Availability: Distributes traffic across multiple instances to improve availability.
- Performance: Improves application performance by reducing response times.
- Scalability: Automatically scales to handle increased traffic.

3. Security Lists:

Security Lists control inbound and outbound traffic to and from instances within a subnet. You can define rules to allow or deny traffic based on source and destination IP addresses, port numbers, and protocols.

Key Features:

- Granular Control: Precise control over network traffic.
- Enhanced Security: Protect your instances from unauthorized access.
- Simplified Security Management: Centralized management of security rules.

By effectively utilizing these networking services, organizations can build highly secure, scalable, and reliable network environments on OCI.

DATABASE SERVICES (Autonomous Database, Database Cloud)

OCI offers a range of database services to meet diverse database needs, including:

1. Autonomous Database:

Autonomous Database is a fully managed database service that automates many database tasks, such as patching, backups, and tuning. It is available in two editions: Autonomous Transaction Processing (ATP) and Autonomous Data Warehouse (ADW).

Key Features:

- Self-Driving: Automated database management tasks.
- High Performance: Optimized performance for various workloads.
- Security: Built-in security features to protect data.
- Scalability: Easily scale database resources up or down.

2. Database Cloud:

Database Cloud is a fully managed database service that provides a variety of database options, including Oracle Database, MySQL, and PostgreSQL. It offers flexibility and choice for organizations with diverse database needs.

Key Features:

- Multiple Database Options: Choose from a variety of database engines.
- Easy Management: Simplified database management with automated tasks.
- High Availability: Ensure high availability and disaster recovery.
- Scalability: Scale database resources to meet changing demands.

By leveraging these database services, organizations can accelerate application development, improve performance, and enhance data security.

PART II: IMPLEMENTING CLOUD-BASED IT SOLUTIONS

CHAPTER 3: PLANNING AND DESIGNING CLOUD SOLUTIONS

IDENTIFYING CLOUD-SUITABLE WORKLOADS

A crucial step in planning and designing cloud solutions is identifying the appropriate workloads to migrate or deploy to the cloud. Not all applications and workloads are suitable for the cloud. To make informed decisions, consider the following factors:

Characteristics of Cloud-Suitable Workloads:

- Scalability: Workloads that experience fluctuating demand, such as web applications or data processing pipelines, are well-suited for the cloud. Cloud providers offer flexible scaling options to accommodate varying workloads.

- Elasticity: Workloads that require rapid scaling up or down in response to sudden changes in demand are ideal for the cloud. Cloud services enable organizations to quickly provision and release resources as needed.

- Standardized Technologies: Workloads that rely on standard technologies and platforms are more easily migrated to the cloud. Cloud providers offer a wide range of standardized services, reducing the need for custom configurations.

- High Availability and Disaster Recovery: Workloads that require high availability and disaster recovery can benefit from the built-in redundancy and fault tolerance of cloud infrastructure.

- Cost-Effectiveness: Workloads with variable costs or those that can benefit from pay-as-you-go pricing models are well-suited for the cloud.

Identifying Cloud-Suitable Workloads:

1. Assess Current Workloads:

- Identify the applications and services that are currently running on-premises.

- Evaluate the performance, scalability, and cost-effectiveness of each workload.

- Consider the potential benefits of migrating to the cloud, such as improved performance, reduced costs, and increased agility.

2. Consider Cloud-Native Applications:

- Evaluate the suitability of designing and developing new applications specifically for the cloud.
- Cloud-native applications can take advantage of cloud-specific features, such as microservices architecture, containerization, and serverless computing.

3. Identify Legacy Workloads:

- Assess the feasibility of migrating legacy workloads to the cloud.
- Consider the potential challenges, such as compatibility issues and modernization efforts.
- Evaluate the cost-benefit analysis of migrating legacy workloads versus re-architecting them for the cloud.

4. Evaluate Security and Compliance Requirements:

- Identify any specific security and compliance requirements for the workloads.
- Assess the cloud provider's security capabilities and compliance certifications.
- Determine if the cloud provider can meet the organization's security and compliance needs.

By carefully identifying cloud-suitable workloads, organizations can maximize the benefits of cloud computing while minimizing risks and costs.

ASSESSING CLOUD READINESS

Once you've identified cloud-suitable workloads, the next step is to assess your organization's readiness for cloud adoption. This involves evaluating various factors, including:

Technical Readiness:

- Infrastructure Assessment: Evaluate your existing IT infrastructure, including hardware, software, and network components.
- Skillset Assessment: Assess the skills and knowledge of your IT team. Do they have the necessary expertise to manage cloud environments?
- Data Center Assessment: Evaluate the readiness of your data center to support cloud migration or hybrid cloud deployments.

Organizational Readiness:

- Business Alignment: Ensure that cloud adoption aligns with your organization's overall business strategy and goals.

- Budget Allocation: Determine the budget required for cloud migration and ongoing operational costs.

- Change Management: Develop a change management plan to address organizational and cultural changes.

- Governance and Security: Establish governance processes and security policies to manage cloud resources effectively.

Key Considerations:

- Cloud Maturity Model: Evaluate your organization's cloud maturity level to identify areas for improvement.

- Vendor Assessment: Select a suitable cloud provider based on your specific needs, such as cost, performance, security, and compliance.

- Risk Assessment: Identify potential risks associated with cloud adoption and develop mitigation strategies.

- Migration Strategy: Develop a migration strategy, including data migration, application migration, and infrastructure migration.

By carefully assessing your organization's readiness, you can mitigate risks and ensure a successful cloud adoption journey.

DESIGNING CLOUD ARCHITECTURES

Designing a robust cloud architecture involves several key considerations:

1. Identify Architectural Patterns:

- Microservices Architecture: Break down applications into smaller, independent services.

- Serverless Architecture: Leverage serverless functions for event-driven and stateless workloads.

- Container-Based Architecture: Use containers to package applications and their dependencies.

2. Choose the Right Cloud Services:

- Select appropriate compute, storage, networking, and database services based on workload requirements.
- Consider factors like performance, scalability, cost-effectiveness, and security.

3. Design for High Availability and Disaster Recovery:

- Implement redundancy and fault tolerance mechanisms.
- Utilize load balancing and auto-scaling to ensure high availability.
- Design disaster recovery strategies, such as backups and failover mechanisms.

4. Optimize for Performance:

- Choose the right instance types and storage options.
- Optimize network configurations to minimize latency.
- Implement caching strategies to improve response times.

5. Ensure Security:

- Implement strong security measures, such as encryption, access controls, and network security.
- Regularly patch and update systems.
- Monitor for security threats and vulnerabilities.

6. Consider Cost Optimization:

- Rightsize resources to avoid overprovisioning.
- Utilize reserved instances and spot instances to reduce costs.
- Implement cost monitoring and optimization strategies.

7. Plan for Scalability:

- Design architectures that can easily scale to accommodate increasing workloads.
- Utilize auto-scaling features to automatically adjust resources based on demand.

By following these guidelines, you can design cloud architectures that are reliable, scalable, and cost-effective.

SECURITY CONSIDERATIONS IN CLOUD ENVIRONMENTS

Security is a paramount concern when adopting cloud computing. Here are some key security considerations:

1. Data Security:

- Encryption: Implement strong encryption techniques to protect data at rest and in transit.
- Data Loss Prevention (DLP): Implement DLP measures to prevent unauthorized data leakage.
- Data Classification and Labeling: Classify data based on sensitivity and apply appropriate security controls.

2. Identity and Access Management (IAM):

- Strong Password Policies: Enforce strong password policies to prevent unauthorized access.
- Multi-Factor Authentication (MFA): Implement MFA to add an extra layer of security.
- Least Privilege Principle: Grant users only the necessary permissions to perform their tasks.
- Regular Access Reviews: Regularly review and revoke unnecessary access privileges.

3. Network Security:

- Network Segmentation: Segment your network into smaller, isolated subnets to limit the impact of potential breaches.
- Firewall Rules: Implement firewall rules to control inbound and outbound traffic.
- Intrusion Detection and Prevention Systems (IDPS): Deploy IDPS to detect and prevent attacks.
- VPN and SSL/TLS: Use VPNs and SSL/TLS to secure remote access.

4. Cloud Security Posture Management (CSPM):

- Continuous Monitoring: Continuously monitor your cloud environment for security threats and vulnerabilities.
- Configuration Management: Ensure that cloud resources are configured securely.

- Security Incident and Event Management (SIEM): Implement SIEM solutions to detect and respond to security incidents.

5. Compliance and Regulations:

- Compliance Frameworks: Adhere to relevant industry standards and regulations, such as GDPR, HIPAA, and PCI DSS.

- Regular Audits and Assessments: Conduct regular security audits and assessments to identify and address vulnerabilities.

By following these security best practices, organizations can mitigate risks and protect their sensitive data in cloud environments.

CHAPTER 4: MIGRATING TO THE CLOUD

MIGRATION STRATEGIES (Lift-and-Shift, Re-Platforming, Re-Architecting)

When migrating applications and data to the cloud, organizations must choose the appropriate migration strategy. The three primary strategies are:

1. Lift-and-Shift:

Lift-and-Shift involves moving existing applications to the cloud with minimal changes. This strategy is suitable for simple applications that do not require significant architectural changes.

Key Characteristics:
- Minimal Changes: Applications are migrated to the cloud without significant modifications.
- Quick Migration: Can be a relatively quick migration process.
- Limited Benefits: May not fully leverage the benefits of the cloud, such as scalability and elasticity.

2. Re-Platforming:

Re-Platforming involves migrating applications to the cloud with some modifications to optimize performance and scalability. This strategy is suitable for applications that can benefit from cloud-native features, such as auto-scaling and load balancing.

Key Characteristics:
- Moderate Changes: Applications are modified to leverage cloud-native features.
- Improved Performance and Scalability: Can improve performance and scalability.
- Reduced Technical Debt: Can reduce technical debt by modernizing the application.

3. Re-Architecting

Re-Architecting involves completely redesigning and rebuilding applications to take full advantage of cloud-native technologies. This strategy is suitable for complex applications that require significant modernization.

Key Characteristics:
- Significant Changes: Applications are redesigned and rebuilt from the ground up.
- Maximum Benefits: Can fully leverage the benefits of the cloud, such as scalability, elasticity, and cost-effectiveness.
- Higher Investment: Requires significant time and resources.

Choosing the Right Strategy:

The choice of migration strategy depends on several factors:

- Application Complexity: Complex applications may require a more comprehensive re-architecture.

- Business Requirements: Consider the specific business needs and priorities.

- Technical Expertise: Assess the organization's technical expertise and resources.

- Cost Constraints: Evaluate the cost implications of each strategy.

- Time Constraints: Consider the desired migration timeline.

By carefully evaluating these factors, organizations can select the most appropriate migration strategy to achieve their cloud migration goals.

MIGRATION TOOLS AND TECHNIQUES

To streamline the migration process, organizations can leverage various tools and techniques:

TOOLS:

Cloud Migration Tools:

- AWS Migration Hub: Facilitates migration to AWS by providing a centralized view of the migration process.

- Azure Migrate: Simplifies migration to Azure by assessing, planning, and executing migrations.

- Oracle Cloud Infrastructure Migration Tools: Offers tools for migrating databases, workloads, and applications to OCI.

Data Migration Tools:

- Database Migration Tools: Migrate databases between different platforms and cloud providers.

- Data Transfer Tools: Transfer large amounts of data efficiently and securely.

Configuration Management Tools:

- Ansible: Automate configuration management and application deployment.

- Puppet: Automate the provisioning and configuration of servers and applications.
- Chef: Automate infrastructure and application configuration.

TECHNIQUES:

- Lift-and-Shift: Use migration tools to lift and shift applications to the cloud with minimal changes.
- Re-Platforming: Use containerization and virtualization technologies to re-platform applications.
- Re-Architecting: Break down monolithic applications into microservices and deploy them on cloud-native platforms.
- Phased Migration: Migrate applications in phases to reduce risk and complexity.
- Pilot Projects: Conduct pilot migrations to test the migration process and identify potential challenges.

BEST PRACTICES:

- Create a Detailed Migration Plan: Develop a comprehensive migration plan that outlines the steps, timelines, and resources required.
- Assess and Optimize Workloads: Identify and optimize workloads for cloud migration.
- Test and Validate: Thoroughly test migrated applications to ensure they function correctly in the cloud environment.
- Monitor and Optimize: Continuously monitor the performance and cost-effectiveness of cloud resources.
- Security and Compliance: Prioritize security and compliance throughout the migration process.

By following these best practices and leveraging appropriate tools and techniques, organizations can successfully migrate their applications and data to the cloud, realizing the benefits of increased agility, scalability, and cost-effectiveness.

CHALLENGES AND BEST PRACTICES FOR CLOUD MIGRATION

Cloud migration, while offering numerous benefits, can also present challenges. Here are some common challenges and best practices to address them:

CHALLENGES:

- Technical Complexity: Migrating complex applications and legacy systems can be technically challenging.

- Security Risks: Ensuring data security and compliance in the cloud requires careful planning and implementation.

- Cost Optimization: Optimizing cloud costs can be complex, and unexpected costs may arise.

- Vendor Lock-in: Relying heavily on a single cloud provider can limit flexibility and increase costs.

- Skill Gap: Organizations may lack the necessary skills to manage and operate cloud environments.

BEST PRACTICES:

- Thorough Planning: Develop a detailed migration plan, including timelines, resource allocation, and risk mitigation strategies.

- Choose the Right Migration Strategy: Select the appropriate migration strategy (lift-and-shift, re-platforming, or re-architecting) based on application complexity and business requirements.

- Assess and Optimize Workloads: Identify cloud-suitable workloads and optimize them for performance and cost-effectiveness.

- Leverage Automation Tools: Use automation tools to streamline the migration process and reduce manual effort.

- Implement Strong Security Measures: Prioritize security throughout the migration process, including data encryption, access controls, and network security.

- Monitor and Optimize Performance: Continuously monitor cloud resources and performance metrics to identify and address issues.

- Establish a Robust Governance Framework: Implement governance policies and procedures to ensure compliance and control.

- Train and Upskill Staff: Provide training and development opportunities to equip your team with the necessary cloud skills.
- Consider a Multi-Cloud Strategy: Diversify your cloud investments to avoid vendor lock-in and optimize costs.

- Regularly Review and Optimize: Continuously review and optimize your cloud environment to ensure it meets your evolving needs.

By addressing these challenges and following best practices, organizations can successfully migrate to the cloud and realize the benefits of this transformative technology.

CHAPTER 5: MANAGING AND OPERATING CLOUD ENVIRONMENTS

OCI CONSOLE AND CLI

Oracle Cloud Infrastructure (OCI) provides two primary interfaces for managing and operating cloud resources: the OCI Console and the OCI CLI.

OCI Console

The OCI Console is a web-based graphical user interface that allows you to manage and monitor your cloud resources. It provides a user-friendly interface with intuitive dashboards and wizards to simplify common tasks.

Key Features of OCI Console:

- Intuitive Dashboard: Visualize the health and performance of your cloud resources.

- Drag-and-Drop Functionality: Easily create and configure resources.

- Role-Based Access Control (RBAC): Control access to resources based on user roles and permissions.

- Monitoring and Logging: Monitor the performance and health of your resources and review logs.

- Automation and Scripting: Automate tasks using scripts and APIs.

OCI CLI

The OCI CLI is a command-line interface that allows you to interact with OCI programmatically. It provides a powerful and flexible way to automate tasks, script complex workflows, and integrate OCI with other tools and systems.

Key Features of OCI CLI:

- Automation: Automate tasks and workflows.

- Scripting: Create custom scripts to automate repetitive tasks.

- Integration: Integrate OCI with other tools and systems.

- Flexibility: Perform complex tasks that may not be possible with the console.

Choosing the Right Tool

The choice between the OCI Console and OCI CLI depends on your specific needs and preferences. Consider the following factors:

- Complexity of Tasks: For simple tasks, the OCI Console is often sufficient. For complex tasks, the OCI CLI offers more flexibility and automation capabilities.

- Automation Needs: If you need to automate repetitive tasks, the OCI CLI is the better choice.

- Integration with Other Tools: The OCI CLI can be integrated with other tools and systems, such as CI/CD pipelines and configuration management tools.

- User Preference: Some users may prefer the visual interface of the OCI Console, while others may prefer the command-line interface of the OCI CLI.

By effectively using both the OCI Console and OCI CLI, you can efficiently manage and operate your OCI environment.

RESOURCE MANAGEMENT AND COST OPTIMIZATION

Effective resource management and cost optimization are crucial for maximizing the value of your cloud investment. Here are some key strategies to consider:

Resource Management

- Rightsizing Instances: Select instance types that are appropriate for your workload's specific needs. Avoid overprovisioning resources, as this can lead to unnecessary costs.

- Auto-Scaling: Use auto-scaling to automatically adjust the number of instances based on demand, ensuring optimal performance and cost-efficiency.

- Spot Instances: Leverage spot instances for cost-effective compute capacity, especially for non-critical workloads.

- Resource Utilization Monitoring: Regularly monitor resource utilization to identify opportunities for optimization.

- Resource Cleanup: Regularly clean up unused resources, such as storage volumes and network security groups.

Cost Optimization

- Reserved Instances: Purchase reserved instances for significant cost savings on consistent workloads.

- Discount Programs: Take advantage of various discount programs offered by cloud providers.

- Cost Allocation Tags: Use tags to track costs and allocate them to specific projects or departments.

- Cost Monitoring and Analysis: Use cloud provider tools to monitor and analyze costs.

- Budgeting and Forecasting: Set budgets and forecasts to control spending.

- Rightsizing and Optimization: Continuously optimize resource utilization and eliminate unnecessary costs.

By implementing these strategies, you can effectively manage your cloud resources and reduce costs while maintaining optimal performance.

MONITORING AND LOGGING

Effective monitoring and logging are essential for ensuring the performance, security, and reliability of cloud environments. OCI provides a comprehensive set of monitoring and logging tools to help you gain insights into your infrastructure and applications.

MONITORING:

- Performance Monitoring: Monitor the performance of your instances, databases, and other resources.

- Alerting: Set up alerts to notify you of potential issues, such as high CPU utilization or disk space shortages.

- Real-Time Metrics: View real-time metrics to identify performance bottlenecks.

- Historical Data: Analyze historical data to identify trends and patterns.

LOGGING:

- Log Analytics: Analyze logs to identify issues, troubleshoot problems, and gain insights into application behavior.

- Log Aggregation: Collect logs from various sources, including instances, databases, and applications.

- Log Filtering and Searching: Filter and search logs to quickly find specific information.
- Log Archiving: Archive logs for long-term retention and compliance.

Key Monitoring and Logging Tools in OCI:

- Oracle Cloud Infrastructure Logging: A fully managed logging service that collects and analyzes logs from various sources.
- Oracle Cloud Infrastructure Monitoring: A comprehensive monitoring service that provides real-time insights into the health and performance of your cloud resources.
- Oracle Management Cloud: A cloud-based management and monitoring solution that provides a unified view of your entire IT infrastructure.

By effectively utilizing these monitoring and logging tools, you can proactively identify and resolve issues, improve performance, and ensure the security and reliability of your cloud environment.

AUTOMATION AND SCRIPTING (Terraform, Ansible)

Automation and scripting are essential for efficient management and deployment of cloud resources. By automating tasks, you can reduce errors, improve consistency, and accelerate deployment times.

TERRAFORM

Terraform is an open-source infrastructure as code (IaC) tool that allows you to define and provision infrastructure resources in a declarative way. With Terraform, you can create, modify, and delete resources using a simple, human-readable configuration language called HashiCorp Configuration Language (HCL).

Key Benefits of Terraform:

- Infrastructure as Code: Treat infrastructure as code, enabling version control, collaboration, and automation.
- Multi-Cloud Support: Manage infrastructure across multiple cloud providers, including OCI, AWS, and Azure.
- Modular Design: Break down infrastructure into reusable modules.
- State File: Maintain the state of your infrastructure, making it easier to manage and recover from failures.

ANSIBLE

Ansible is an open-source automation platform that simplifies IT automation tasks. It uses a simple, agentless approach to manage and configure systems.

Key Benefits of Ansible:

- Agentless Architecture: No need to install agents on target systems.

- Playbooks: Define automation tasks in YAML-based playbooks.

- Idempotency: Ensures that tasks are performed consistently, avoiding unintended changes.

- Modules: A vast library of modules for various tasks, such as provisioning servers, deploying applications, and configuring networks.

Combining Terraform and Ansible

Terraform and Ansible can be used together to create powerful automation workflows. Terraform can be used to provision infrastructure, and Ansible can be used to configure and deploy applications on that infrastructure.

By leveraging automation and scripting tools like Terraform and Ansible, you can significantly improve the efficiency and reliability of your cloud operations.

DISASTER RECOVERY AND BUSINESS CONTINUITY

Disaster recovery and business continuity are critical aspects of cloud strategy. They ensure that your applications and data remain accessible and operational in the event of disruptions such as natural disasters, cyberattacks, or hardware failures.

Key Strategies for Disaster Recovery and Business Continuity:

Data Backup and Recovery:

- Implement regular backups of your data to ensure data integrity and recoverability.

- Utilize cloud-native backup services to automate the backup process.

- Test your backup and recovery procedures regularly to validate their effectiveness.

Disaster Recovery Planning:

- Develop a comprehensive disaster recovery plan that outlines procedures for responding to incidents.
- Define roles and responsibilities for different team members.
- Test your disaster recovery plan regularly to identify and address potential issues.

Business Continuity Planning:

- Develop a business continuity plan that outlines strategies for maintaining critical business functions during disruptions.
- Identify critical business processes and prioritize their recovery.
- Establish alternative work arrangements, such as remote work or business continuity sites.

Multi-Region Deployment:

- Deploy your applications across multiple regions to improve fault tolerance and reduce the impact of regional outages.
- Use load balancing to distribute traffic across multiple regions.

Failover and Failback Mechanisms:

- Implement failover mechanisms to automatically switch to redundant systems in case of failures.
- Plan for failback procedures to restore normal operations after a disaster.

By implementing these strategies, you can minimize the impact of potential disruptions and ensure the continuity of your business operations.

PART III: ADVANCED TOPICS IN ORACLE CLOUD

CHAPTER 6: SECURITY IN THE CLOUD

IDENTITY AND ACCESS MANAGEMENT (IAM)

Identity and Access Management (IAM) is a critical aspect of cloud security. It involves managing user identities, assigning appropriate permissions, and controlling access to resources. Strong IAM practices help protect your cloud environment from unauthorized access and data breaches.

Key Components of IAM:

1. Identity Providers:

- Centralized Identity Providers: Use a centralized identity provider like Oracle Identity Cloud Service (IDCS) to manage user identities and authentication.

- Federated Identity Providers: Leverage federated identity providers like SAML or OAuth to enable single sign-on (SSO) across multiple applications.

2. Access Control:

- Role-Based Access Control (RBAC): Assign roles to users based on their job functions and responsibilities.

- Policy-Based Access Control (PBAC): Define policies to control access to resources based on specific conditions.

- Attribute-Based Access Control (ABAC): Grant access based on user attributes, such as job title, department, or location.

3. Authentication and Authorization:

- Strong Authentication: Use multi-factor authentication (MFA) to enhance security.

- Password Policies: Enforce strong password policies to prevent unauthorized access.

- Session Management: Implement session timeouts and other security measures to protect user sessions.

4. Privileged Access Management (PAM):

- Least Privilege Principle: Grant users only the minimum necessary privileges to perform their tasks.

- Just-in-Time (JIT) Access: Provide temporary access to privileged accounts when needed.

- Session Monitoring and Recording: Monitor and record privileged sessions to detect and prevent malicious activity.

Best Practices for IAM:

- Regularly Review and Update Access Permissions: Ensure that users have the appropriate access levels and revoke unnecessary permissions.

- Implement Strong Password Policies: Enforce strong password policies, including password complexity and expiration requirements.

- Enable MFA: Use MFA to add an extra layer of security to user authentication.

- Monitor for Security Threats: Use security monitoring tools to detect and respond to security threats.

- Stay Updated with Security Best Practices: Stay informed about the latest security threats and vulnerabilities.

- Conduct Regular Security Audits: Conduct regular security audits to identify and address security weaknesses.

By implementing effective IAM practices, you can significantly enhance the security of your cloud environment.

NETWORK SECURITY (Firewalls, Security Lists, VPNs)

Network security is crucial for protecting your cloud environment from unauthorized access and cyberattacks. Here are some key network security considerations:

FIREWALLS:

- Network Firewalls: Filter network traffic based on defined rules to protect your network from unauthorized access.

- Web Application Firewalls (WAFs): Protect web applications from attacks such as SQL injection and cross-site scripting (XSS).

SECURITY LISTS:

- Ingress and Egress Rules: Define rules to control inbound and outbound traffic to your instances.

- Source/Destination IP Ranges: Specify the IP addresses or IP ranges that are allowed to communicate with your instances.

- Port Ranges and Protocols: Control the ports and protocols that are allowed.

VPNS:

- Site-to-Site VPNs: Connect your on-premises network to your cloud network.

- Client VPNs: Allow remote users to securely access your cloud resources.

- IPsec and SSL/TLS: Use industry-standard encryption protocols to secure VPN connections.

Additional Network Security Best Practices:

- Network Segmentation: Divide your network into smaller, isolated segments to limit the impact of potential breaches.

- Intrusion Detection and Prevention Systems (IDPS): Monitor network traffic for malicious activity and take appropriate actions.

- Regular Security Assessments: Conduct regular security assessments to identify and address vulnerabilities.

- Network Access Control (NAC): Enforce strict access controls to limit access to network resources.

- Secure Remote Access: Implement secure remote access solutions, such as VPNs and virtual desktop infrastructure (VDI).

By implementing these network security measures, you can significantly enhance the security of your cloud environment.

DATA SECURITY AND ENCRYPTION

Data security is paramount in cloud environments. Protecting sensitive data from unauthorized access, theft, and data breaches is essential. Here are some key data security and encryption practices:

DATA ENCRYPTION:

- Data Encryption at Rest: Encrypt data stored on disk or in object storage to protect it from unauthorized access.

- Data Encryption in Transit: Encrypt data transmitted over the network to prevent interception.

- Key Management: Use strong key management practices to protect encryption keys.

Data Loss Prevention (DLP):

- Data Classification: Classify data based on sensitivity levels to apply appropriate security controls.

- Data Access Controls: Implement strict access controls to limit access to sensitive data.

- Data Loss Prevention Tools: Use DLP tools to monitor and control data movement.

Data Backup and Recovery:

- Regular Backups: Regularly back up your data to protect against data loss.

- Data Retention Policies: Implement data retention policies to comply with regulatory requirements and minimize storage costs.

- Disaster Recovery Planning: Develop a comprehensive disaster recovery plan to ensure business continuity.

Additional Data Security Best Practices:

- Regular Security Assessments: Conduct regular security assessments to identify and address vulnerabilities.

- Security Awareness Training: Educate employees about security best practices.

- Incident Response Plan: Develop an incident response plan to respond to security incidents promptly and effectively.

- Third-Party Risk Management: Assess the security practices of third-party providers.

By implementing these data security and encryption practices, you can protect your sensitive data from unauthorized access, theft, and data breaches.

THREAT DETECTION AND RESPONSE

Effective threat detection and response is essential to protect your cloud environment from cyberattacks. By implementing robust security measures and monitoring tools, you can identify and respond to threats promptly.

Key Threat Detection and Response Strategies:

1. **Security Information and Event Management (SIEM):**

   - Centralize and correlate security logs from various sources.
   - Detect anomalies and security threats.
   - Generate alerts for potential security incidents.

2. **Intrusion Detection and Prevention Systems (IDPS):**

   - Monitor network traffic for malicious activity.
   - Detect and block attacks in real-time.

3. **Vulnerability Scanning:**

   - Identify and assess vulnerabilities in your systems and applications.
   - Prioritize vulnerabilities based on severity and risk.

4. **Web Application Firewalls (WAFs):**

   - Protect web applications from attacks such as SQL injection and cross-site scripting (XSS).

5. **Incident Response Planning:**

   - Develop a comprehensive incident response plan to guide your response to security incidents.
   - Establish incident response teams and define roles and responsibilities.
   - Conduct regular incident response drills to test your plan.

Best Practices for Threat Detection and Response:

- Stay Informed: Stay up-to-date with the latest security threats and vulnerabilities.
- Implement Strong Password Policies: Enforce strong password policies to prevent unauthorized access.
- Use Multi-Factor Authentication (MFA): Add an extra layer of security to user authentication.
- Monitor Network Traffic: Monitor network traffic for suspicious activity.
- Regularly Patch Systems: Keep systems and applications up-to-date with the latest security patches.
- Conduct Regular Security Audits: Conduct regular security audits to identify and address vulnerabilities.

By implementing these threat detection and response strategies, you can significantly enhance the security of your cloud environment and minimize the impact of potential cyberattacks.

CHAPTER 7: DATABASE AND ANALYTICS

AUTONOMOUS DATABASE

Oracle Autonomous Database is a fully automated, self-driving database service that eliminates the need for manual database administration tasks. It offers a high-performance, scalable, and secure database platform, freeing up IT teams to focus on strategic initiatives.

Key Features of Autonomous Database:

- Self-Driving: Automates routine database tasks such as patching, backups, and tuning.
- High Performance: Delivers high performance and scalability for both transactional and analytical workloads.
- Security: Provides robust security features, including encryption, access control, and threat detection.
- Always-On Availability: Ensures high availability and minimal downtime.
- Self-Repairing: Automatically detects and repairs issues, minimizing downtime.

Use Cases for Autonomous Database:

- Enterprise Applications: Power mission-critical applications with high performance and reliability.
- Data Warehousing and Analytics: Analyze large datasets and gain valuable insights.
- IoT and Big Data: Handle massive volumes of data from IoT devices and other sources.
- Machine Learning and AI: Train and deploy machine learning models on a scalable and secure platform.

Benefits of Using Autonomous Database:

- Reduced Administrative Overhead: Automates routine tasks, freeing up IT teams to focus on strategic initiatives.
- Improved Performance: Delivers high performance and scalability.
- Enhanced Security: Provides robust security features to protect sensitive data.
- Increased Productivity: Accelerates development and deployment of applications.

- Lower Costs: Reduces operational costs and minimizes downtime.

DATA WAREHOUSE CLOUD

Oracle Data Warehouse Cloud is a fully managed, high-performance data warehouse service that simplifies data warehousing and analytics. It provides a scalable, secure, and cost-effective platform for storing and analyzing large datasets.

Key Features of Data Warehouse Cloud:

- Self-Service Analytics: Enables business users to perform ad-hoc analysis without requiring technical expertise.

- Scalability: Easily scale the data warehouse to accommodate growing data volumes and increasing user demands.

- Performance: Delivers high performance for complex queries and data loads.

- Security: Provides robust security features to protect sensitive data.

- Integration: Integrates seamlessly with other Oracle Cloud services, such as Analytics Cloud and Data Integration.

Benefits of Using Data Warehouse Cloud:

- Accelerated Time to Insights: Quickly analyze large datasets and gain valuable insights.

- Improved Decision-Making: Make data-driven decisions with confidence.

- Reduced Operational Costs: Eliminate the need for managing complex data warehouse infrastructure.

- Enhanced Productivity: Empower business users to perform self-service analysis.

- Enhanced Security: Protect sensitive data with advanced security features.

ANALYTICS CLOUD

Oracle Analytics Cloud is a comprehensive cloud-based analytics platform that empowers users to discover insights, make data-driven decisions, and improve business performance. It provides a range of analytics capabilities, including data visualization, predictive analytics, and machine learning.

Key Features of Analytics Cloud:

- Data Visualization: Create interactive dashboards and visualizations to explore data and uncover insights.

- Predictive Analytics: Build predictive models to forecast future trends and make informed decisions.

- Machine Learning: Leverage machine learning algorithms to automate data analysis and extract valuable insights.

- Data Preparation and Integration: Easily prepare and integrate data from various sources.

- Collaboration: Share insights and collaborate with others through a centralized platform.

Benefits of Using Analytics Cloud:

- Accelerated Time to Insights: Quickly analyze large datasets and gain actionable insights.

- Improved Decision-Making: Make data-driven decisions with confidence.

- Enhanced Productivity: Empower business users to perform self-service analysis.

- Increased Innovation: Drive innovation by leveraging advanced analytics capabilities.

- Reduced Time to Market: Accelerate the development and deployment of data-driven applications.

MACHINE LEARNING AND AI SERVICES

Oracle offers a comprehensive suite of machine learning and AI services to help organizations extract insights from data and build intelligent applications.

Key Machine Learning and AI Services:

1. Machine Learning in Oracle Database:

- Enables data scientists to build, train, and deploy machine learning models directly within the database.

- Provides a range of algorithms, including regression, classification, clustering, and time series forecasting.

- Supports popular programming languages like Python and R.

2. AI and Machine Learning Services:

- Offers pre-built AI and machine learning models for tasks such as image recognition, natural language processing, and anomaly detection.

- Provides a low-code/no-code interface for building and deploying machine learning models.

- Enables customization of pre-built models to meet specific business needs.

3. Autonomous Database with Machine Learning:

- Integrates machine learning capabilities directly into the database.

- Automates data preparation, feature engineering, and model training.

- Provides insights and predictions without requiring complex data science expertise.

Benefits of Oracle's Machine Learning and AI Services:

- Accelerated Time to Insights: Quickly build, train, and deploy machine learning models.

- Improved Decision-Making: Leverage AI-powered insights to make informed decisions.

- Enhanced Productivity: Automate routine tasks and streamline workflows.

- Increased Innovation: Drive innovation with advanced AI and machine learning capabilities.

- Scalability: Handle large datasets and complex models with ease.

By leveraging Oracle's machine learning and AI services, organizations can unlock the value of their data and gain a competitive edge.

CHAPTER 8: SERVERLESS COMPUTING

FUNCTIONS AS A SERVICE (FAAS)

Functions as a Service (FaaS) is a serverless computing model that allows you to build and deploy applications without managing the underlying infrastructure. With FaaS, you write and deploy small, independent functions that are triggered by events, such as HTTP requests, database changes, or messages from a message queue.

Key Benefits of FaaS:

- Serverless: No need to manage servers or infrastructure.
- Pay-Per-Use: Pay only for the resources consumed, making it cost-effective for applications with variable workloads.
- Scalability: Automatically scale your applications to handle increased traffic.
- Rapid Development and Deployment: Quickly develop, test, and deploy functions.
- High Availability: Built-in redundancy and fault tolerance.

Common Use Cases for FaaS:

- Data Processing: Process large amounts of data in real-time or batch.
- Web Applications: Build and deploy web applications without managing servers.
- IoT Applications: Process data from IoT devices and trigger actions.
- Mobile Backends: Develop scalable and reliable backends for mobile applications.

Popular FaaS Platforms:

- Oracle Functions: A fully managed serverless platform on Oracle Cloud Infrastructure.
- AWS Lambda: A serverless computing platform offered by Amazon Web Services.
- Azure Functions: A serverless computing platform offered by Microsoft Azure.
- Google Cloud Functions: A serverless computing platform offered by Google Cloud Platform.

CONTAINER-BASED SERVICES

Container-based services offer a powerful way to package and deploy applications in a consistent and portable manner. Containers provide a lightweight, standalone environment that includes everything needed to run an application, such as code, libraries, and system tools.

Key Benefits of Container-Based Services:

- Portability: Containers can be deployed consistently across different environments.

- Scalability: Easily scale applications up or down to meet changing demands.

- Isolation: Containers provide isolation between applications, improving security and reliability.

- Efficient Resource Utilization: Containers share the host operating system kernel, reducing resource overhead.

Popular Container-Based Services:

- Oracle Container Engine for Kubernetes (OKE): A fully managed Kubernetes service on Oracle Cloud Infrastructure.

- Kubernetes: An open-source platform for managing containerized applications.

- Docker: A platform for building, shipping, and running containers.

Key Considerations for Container-Based Services:

- Container Orchestration: Use a container orchestration platform like Kubernetes to manage and scale containerized applications.

- Security: Implement strong security measures to protect containerized applications.

- Networking: Configure network connectivity between containers and external services.

- Monitoring and Logging: Monitor the performance and health of containerized applications.

- Storage: Manage persistent storage for containerized applications.

By leveraging container-based services, organizations can accelerate application development, improve deployment efficiency, and enhance scalability and reliability.

CHAPTER 9: INTEGRATION AND API MANAGEMENT

INTEGRATION CLOUD

Oracle Integration Cloud is a powerful integration platform as a service (iPaaS) that enables you to connect applications, data, and processes across your organization and with external systems. It simplifies integration tasks, accelerates application development, and improves overall business efficiency.

Key Features of Integration Cloud:

- Pre-built Connectors: A wide range of pre-built connectors to popular applications and services.

- Visual Integration Designer: A drag-and-drop interface for designing and building integration flows.

- API Management: Manage, secure, and govern APIs.

- Data Integration: Extract, transform, and load (ETL) data between different systems.

- Process Automation: Automate business processes and workflows.

- Event-Driven Architecture: Trigger integrations based on events from various sources.

Benefits of Using Integration Cloud:

- Accelerated Integration: Quickly connect applications and data sources.

- Improved Efficiency: Automate business processes and reduce manual effort.

- Enhanced Data Quality: Ensure data consistency and accuracy.

- Increased Agility: Respond to changing business needs quickly.

- Enhanced Security: Securely integrate systems and protect sensitive data.

API PLATFORM CLOUD

Oracle API Platform Cloud is a comprehensive API management platform that enables you to design, build, secure, and manage APIs. It provides a centralized platform for API creation, governance, and consumption.

Key Features of API Platform Cloud:

- API Design:** Design APIs using industry standards like OpenAPI Specification (formerly Swagger).

- API Development:** Build and test APIs using a variety of programming languages and frameworks.

- API Security: Secure APIs with authentication, authorization, and encryption.

- API Gateway: Route and manage API traffic, enforce rate limits, and protect against attacks.

- API Analytics: Monitor API usage, performance, and error rates.

- Developer Portal: Provide a self-service portal for developers to discover and consume APIs.

Benefits of Using API Platform Cloud:

- Accelerated API Development: Quickly design, build, and deploy APIs.

- Improved API Security: Protect APIs from unauthorized access and security threats.

- Enhanced Developer Experience: Provide a seamless developer experience with a self-service portal.

- Increased API Adoption: Promote API adoption and reuse within and outside the organization.

- Better API Management: Gain visibility into API usage and performance.

By leveraging API Platform Cloud, organizations can accelerate digital transformation, enable innovation, and create new revenue streams through API-driven business models.

PART IV: REAL-WORLD USE CASES AND BEST PRACTICES

CHAPTER 10: CASE STUDY: MIGRATING A TRADITIONAL DATA CENTER TO OCI

CHALLENGES AND CONSIDERATIONS

Migrating a traditional data center to Oracle Cloud Infrastructure (OCI) can be a complex process. Several challenges and considerations must be addressed to ensure a successful migration:

CHALLENGES:

1. Technical Complexity:

- Legacy Systems: Migrating legacy systems that may not be cloud-native can be challenging.

- Network Complexity: Migrating complex network configurations, especially those with specialized hardware, can be complex.

- Data Migration: Migrating large volumes of data can be time-consuming and requires careful planning.

2. Security Concerns:

- Data Security: Ensuring the security of sensitive data during migration and in the cloud is critical.

- Access Control: Implementing strong access controls to protect cloud resources is essential.

- Compliance: Adhering to industry regulations and compliance standards.

3. Cost Optimization:

- Rightsizing Resources: Selecting the appropriate instance types and storage options to optimize costs.

- Cost Monitoring: Continuously monitoring cloud usage and identifying opportunities for cost reduction.

- Reserved Instances: Leveraging reserved instances to reduce costs.

4. Organizational Change Management:

- Skill Gap: Ensuring that the organization has the necessary skills to manage cloud environments.

- Cultural Shift: Adopting a cloud-first mindset and embracing new ways of working.

- Process Reengineering: Rethinking processes to take advantage of cloud capabilities.

CONSIDERATIONS:

1. Workload Assessment:

- Identifying workloads suitable for migration to the cloud.
- Assessing the complexity and dependencies of each workload.
- Prioritizing workloads based on business impact and technical feasibility.

2. Cloud Strategy:

- Defining a clear cloud strategy that aligns with business goals.
- Choosing the appropriate cloud migration strategy (lift-and-shift, re-platforming, or re-architecting).
- Developing a migration plan with detailed timelines and milestones.

3. Security and Compliance:

- Implementing robust security measures, such as encryption, access controls, and network security.
- Ensuring compliance with industry regulations and standards.
- Conducting regular security assessments and vulnerability scans.

4. Cost Management:

- Developing a cost optimization strategy.
- Using cost monitoring tools to track cloud usage and identify cost-saving opportunities.
- Implementing cost allocation and budgeting practices.

MIGRATION STEPS AND BEST PRACTICES

Migration Steps:

1. Assess Current Infrastructure:

- Inventory hardware, software, and network components.
- Identify dependencies and potential challenges.
- Evaluate the suitability of workloads for cloud migration.

2. Choose a Migration Strategy:

- Select the appropriate migration strategy (lift-and-shift, re-platforming, or re-architecting) for each workload.
- Consider factors such as complexity, cost, and time constraints.

3. Prepare the Target Environment:

- Set up the target OCI environment, including virtual networks, security groups, and storage.
- Configure network connectivity between on-premises and cloud environments.
- Ensure that the target environment meets the requirements of the migrated workloads.

4. Migrate Data and Applications:

- Use appropriate data migration tools to transfer data to the cloud.
- Migrate applications using the chosen migration strategy.
- Test migrated applications to ensure they function correctly in the cloud environment.

5. Configure and Optimize:

- Configure cloud resources to optimize performance and cost-effectiveness.
- Implement monitoring and alerting to track the health and performance of cloud resources.
- Optimize network configurations to minimize latency and maximize throughput.

6. Test and Validate:

- Thoroughly test migrated applications to ensure they function correctly in the cloud environment.
- Conduct performance testing to identify and address any performance bottlenecks.
- Validate security configurations to protect sensitive data.

7. Cutover and Transition:

- Plan a cutover strategy to minimize downtime and disruption.
- Coordinate with stakeholders to ensure a smooth transition.
- Test the cutover process to identify and address potential issues.

Best Practices:

1. **Plan Thoroughly:** Develop a detailed migration plan, including timelines, resource allocation, and risk mitigation strategies.

2. **Start Small:** Begin with a pilot migration to test the process and identify potential challenges.

3. **Use Automation Tools:** Leverage automation tools to streamline the migration process and reduce manual effort.

4. **Monitor and Optimize:** Continuously monitor cloud resources and optimize performance and cost-effectiveness.

5. **Security First:** Prioritize security throughout the migration process.

6. **Collaborate with Cloud Provider:** Work closely with Oracle to leverage their expertise and support.

7. **Train and Upskill Staff:** Provide training and development opportunities to ensure your team has the necessary cloud skills.

8. **Regularly Review and Optimize:** Continuously review and optimize your cloud environment to ensure it meets your evolving needs.

LESSONS LEARNED

Migrating a traditional data center to OCI can be a complex and challenging undertaking. However, by learning from the experiences of others, organizations can avoid common pitfalls and ensure a successful migration.

Here are some key lessons learned from real-world migrations:

1. Thorough Planning is Crucial:

- Develop a detailed migration plan that outlines the steps, timelines, and resources required.
- Identify potential challenges and risks, and develop mitigation strategies.
- Regularly review and update the migration plan as needed.

2. Start Small and Iterate:

- Begin with a pilot migration to test the process and identify potential issues.
- Gradually migrate workloads in phases to minimize risk.
- Continuously learn and adapt your approach based on the lessons learned.

3. Leverage Automation:

- Use automation tools to streamline the migration process and reduce manual effort.
- Automate tasks such as provisioning resources, configuring networks, and deploying applications.

4. Prioritize Security:

- Implement strong security measures to protect data and applications in the cloud.
- Conduct regular security assessments and vulnerability scans.
- Stay up-to-date with the latest security best practices.

5. Optimize Costs:

- Rightsize resources to avoid overprovisioning.
- Use cost optimization tools to identify and eliminate unnecessary costs.
- Leverage reserved instances and spot instances to reduce costs.

6. Train and Upskill Staff:

- Provide training and development opportunities to ensure your team has the necessary cloud skills.
- Foster a cloud-native culture within your organization.

7. Monitor and Optimize:

- Continuously monitor the performance and cost-effectiveness of your cloud resources.
- Identify and address performance bottlenecks and security vulnerabilities.
- Optimize resource utilization to reduce costs.

By applying these lessons learned, organizations can successfully migrate their traditional data centers to OCI and realize the benefits of cloud computing.

CHAPTER 11: BUILDING A SCALABLE WEB APPLICATION ON OCI

ARCHITECTURE DESIGN

When designing a scalable web application on OCI, a well-architected solution is crucial. Here's a breakdown of key architectural considerations:

Core Components:

1. Compute:

- Virtual Machines (VMs): Suitable for traditional applications and workloads that require precise control over hardware.

- Bare Metal Instances: Ideal for high-performance workloads like HPC and database servers.

- Functions as a Service (FaaS): Best for event-driven, stateless functions.

- Container Engine for Kubernetes (OKE): For managing and scaling containerized applications.

2. Storage:

- Block Storage: For high-performance, low-latency storage needs.

- Object Storage: For storing large amounts of unstructured data, such as images, videos, and logs.

- File Storage: For sharing files across multiple instances.

3. Networking:

- Virtual Cloud Networks (VCNs): Create isolated networks to segment workloads and improve security.

- Load Balancing: Distribute traffic across multiple instances to improve performance and availability.

- Security Lists: Control inbound and outbound traffic to instances.

4. Database:

- Autonomous Database: A fully managed database service that automates many database tasks.

- Database Cloud: A flexible database service that offers various database engines.

Architectural Patterns:

1. Microservices Architecture:

- Break down the application into smaller, independent services.
- Each service can be scaled independently.
- Improves fault isolation and enables easier updates.

2. Serverless Architecture:
- Use FaaS to build event-driven applications without managing servers.
- Ideal for functions that are triggered by events, such as API calls or data changes.

3. Container-Based Architecture:

- Package applications and dependencies into containers.
- Deploy and manage containers using Kubernetes.
- Provides portability and scalability.

Key Design Considerations:

- Scalability: Design the application to handle increasing traffic and data volumes.

- Performance: Optimize database queries, network configurations, and application code.

- Security: Implement strong security measures, including encryption, access controls, and vulnerability scanning.

- High Availability: Design for redundancy and fault tolerance.

- Cost-Efficiency: Choose the right resources and optimize costs.

- Monitoring and Logging: Implement monitoring and logging to track performance and identify issues.

DEPLOYMENT AND CONFIGURATION

Once the architecture is designed, the next step is to deploy and configure the application on OCI. Here are some key considerations:

DEPLOYMENT STRATEGIES:

- Manual Deployment: Deploy applications manually using the OCI Console or CLI. Suitable for small-scale deployments.

- Automated Deployment: Use automation tools like Terraform, Ansible, or OCI DevOps to automate the deployment process.

- Continuous Integration/Continuous Delivery (CI/CD): Implement a CI/CD pipeline to automate the build, test, and deployment process.

CONFIGURATION MANAGEMENT:

- Configuration Management Tools: Use tools like Ansible, Puppet, or Chef to automate configuration management.

- Infrastructure as Code (IaC): Define infrastructure as code using tools like Terraform to ensure consistency and repeatability.

- Secret Management: Securely store and manage sensitive information, such as API keys and passwords.

Key Configuration Considerations:

- Network Configuration: Configure network security groups, security lists, and route tables to control traffic flow.

- Database Configuration: Optimize database performance by tuning parameters and indexing.

- Application Configuration: Configure application settings, such as environment variables and connection strings.

- Logging and Monitoring: Set up logging and monitoring to track application performance and identify issues.

Best Practices:

- Use Infrastructure as Code: Define infrastructure as code to automate deployment and configuration.

- Implement Continuous Integration and Continuous Delivery: Automate the build, test, and deployment process.

- Monitor and Optimize: Continuously monitor application performance and optimize resource utilization.

- Test Thoroughly: Test applications in different environments to identify and fix issues.
- Plan for Scalability: Design the application to scale horizontally and vertically.
- Consider Security: Implement security best practices, such as encryption, access controls, and vulnerability scanning.

PERFORMANCE OPTIMIZATION AND MONITORING

Optimizing performance and monitoring the health of your web application is crucial for delivering a seamless user experience. Here are some key strategies:

PERFORMANCE OPTIMIZATION:

1. Frontend Optimization:

- Minify and Compress Assets: Reduce file sizes of HTML, CSS, and JavaScript files.
- Optimize Images: Compress images and use appropriate formats.
- Leverage Browser Caching: Enable browser caching to reduce server load and improve page load times.
- Minimize HTTP Requests: Combine and minify CSS and JavaScript files.

2. Backend Optimization:

- Database Optimization: Optimize database queries, indexes, and connections.
- Caching: Implement caching strategies to reduce database load.
- Asynchronous Processing: Use asynchronous tasks for long-running processes.
- Load Balancing: Distribute traffic across multiple instances to improve performance and scalability.

3. Network Optimization:

- Reduce Latency: Minimize network hops and use Content Delivery Networks (CDNs) to reduce latency.
- Optimize DNS: Configure DNS settings to improve DNS resolution times.

MONITORING:

1. **Application Performance Monitoring (APM):**

    - Monitor application performance metrics, such as response times, error rates, and resource utilization.
    - Identify performance bottlenecks and optimize accordingly.

2. **Infrastructure Monitoring:**

    - Monitor the health and performance of infrastructure components, such as servers, databases, and networks.
    - Use tools like OCI Monitoring to track metrics like CPU utilization, memory usage, and disk I/O.

3. **Log Analysis:**

    - Analyze logs to identify errors, exceptions, and performance issues.
    - Use log aggregation and analysis tools to gain insights into application behavior.

Best Practices for Performance Optimization and Monitoring:

- Continuous Monitoring: Monitor application performance and infrastructure health regularly.

- Performance Testing: Conduct regular performance tests to identify bottlenecks and optimize performance.

- A/B Testing: Test different configurations and optimizations to determine the best approach.

- Use Performance Optimization Tools: Leverage tools like profiling tools and code analyzers.

- Optimize for Mobile Devices: Ensure your application is optimized for mobile devices.

- Implement a Robust Error Handling Strategy: Handle errors gracefully and provide informative error messages.

By following these strategies and best practices, you can build and maintain a high-performance web application on OCI.

CHAPTER 12: IMPLEMENTING A DATA LAKE AND DATA WAREHOUSE ON OCI

DATA INGESTION AND TRANSFORMATION

Data ingestion and transformation are crucial steps in building a data lake and data warehouse on OCI. These processes involve collecting data from various sources, cleaning and transforming it, and loading it into the data lake or data warehouse.

DATA INGESTION:

Data Sources:

- On-Premises Data: Data residing in on-premises databases, files, or applications.
- Cloud Data: Data stored in other cloud services or platforms.
- Real-time Data: Data generated by IoT devices, sensors, or streaming applications.
- Social Media Data: Data from social media platforms like Twitter, Facebook, and Instagram.

Ingestion Methods:

- Batch Processing: Process large volumes of data in batches.
- Stream Processing: Process data in real-time as it is generated.
- API-Based Integration: Extract data from APIs and integrate it into the data lake or data warehouse.

Ingestion Tools:

- Oracle Data Integration (ODI): A powerful ETL tool for data integration and transformation.
- Oracle Data Integrator (ODI): A cloud-based ETL tool for data integration and transformation.
- Oracle Data Integrator for Big Data: A cloud-based ETL tool for big data integration.

DATA TRANSFORMATION:

- Data Cleaning: Remove errors, inconsistencies, and duplicates from the data.

- Data Validation: Ensure data quality and consistency.

- Data Enrichment: Add context and meaning to data by combining it with other data sources.

- Data Transformation: Convert data into a suitable format for analysis.

Key Considerations:

- Data Quality: Ensure data quality by implementing data validation and cleansing processes.

- Data Security: Protect sensitive data with encryption and access controls.

- Scalability: Design the data ingestion and transformation pipeline to handle increasing data volumes.

- Performance: Optimize data ingestion and transformation processes to minimize latency.

- Cost-Effectiveness: Choose the right tools and techniques to optimize costs.

DATA ANALYSIS AND VISUALIZATION

Once data is ingested and transformed, the next step is to analyze and visualize it to extract valuable insights.

DATA ANALYSIS:

- SQL: Use SQL to query and analyze data stored in relational databases.

- Python: Leverage Python libraries like Pandas, NumPy, and SciPy for data analysis and manipulation.

- R: A powerful statistical programming language for data analysis and visualization.

- Machine Learning: Apply machine learning algorithms to uncover patterns and make predictions.

DATA VISUALIZATION:

- Oracle Analytics Cloud: A comprehensive analytics platform for data visualization, reporting, and predictive analytics.

- Oracle Data Visualization: Create interactive dashboards and visualizations to explore data.

- Python Libraries: Use libraries like Matplotlib, Seaborn, and Plotly to create custom visualizations.

Key Considerations:

- Data Governance: Implement data governance policies to ensure data quality and security.

- Data Security: Protect sensitive data with appropriate security measures.

- User Experience: Design user-friendly dashboards and visualizations.

- Performance: Optimize queries and visualizations for performance.

- Collaboration: Enable collaboration among data analysts and business users.

DATA SECURITY AND GOVERNANCE

Data security and governance are critical aspects of managing a data lake and data warehouse. Implementing robust security measures and governance policies is essential to protect sensitive data and ensure data quality and integrity.

DATA SECURITY:

- Access Control: Implement strong access controls to limit access to sensitive data.

- Data Encryption: Encrypt data at rest and in transit to protect it from unauthorized access.

- Network Security: Secure network connections to the data lake and data warehouse.

- Data Loss Prevention (DLP): Implement DLP policies to prevent data loss and unauthorized data transfers.

- Regular Security Audits: Conduct regular security audits to identify and address vulnerabilities.

DATA GOVERNANCE:

- Data Quality: Implement data quality standards and processes to ensure data accuracy and consistency.

- Data Lineage: Track the origin and transformation of data to improve data understanding and accountability.

- Data Retention Policies: Define data retention policies to manage data lifecycle and comply with regulations.

- Data Privacy and Compliance: Adhere to data privacy regulations, such as GDPR and CCPA.

- Data Governance Framework: Establish a data governance framework to define roles, responsibilities, and processes.

Key Considerations:

- Data Sensitivity:** Classify data based on sensitivity levels to apply appropriate security measures.

- Data Privacy:** Protect personal and sensitive data in compliance with regulations.

- Data Security Best Practices:** Follow industry best practices for data security.

- Regular Monitoring and Auditing:** Monitor data access and usage to identify and address security threats.

- Incident Response Plan:** Develop a comprehensive incident response plan to respond to security incidents.

By implementing strong data security and governance measures, organizations can protect their valuable data assets and ensure compliance with regulations.

APPENDIX A: OCI CERTIFICATIONS

Oracle Cloud Infrastructure (OCI) Certifications

Oracle offers a range of certifications to validate your expertise in OCI. These certifications can help you advance your career, demonstrate your skills, and increase your earning potential.

Here are some of the popular OCI certifications:

FOUNDATIONAL CERTIFICATIONS:

- Oracle Cloud Infrastructure Foundations Associate: This certification validates your foundational knowledge of OCI, including core services, security, and networking.

ASSOCIATE-LEVEL CERTIFICATIONS:

- Oracle Cloud Infrastructure 2023 Cloud Operations Associate: This certification validates your skills in managing and operating OCI environments.

- Oracle Cloud Infrastructure 2023 Architect Associate: This certification validates your ability to design and implement cloud solutions on OCI.

PROFESSIONAL-LEVEL CERTIFICATIONS:

- Oracle Cloud Infrastructure 2023 Cloud Operations Specialist: This certification validates your advanced skills in managing and operating complex OCI environments.

- Oracle Cloud Infrastructure 2023 Architect Professional: This certification validates your expertise in designing and implementing advanced cloud solutions on OCI.

SPECIALIZED CERTIFICATIONS:

- Oracle Cloud Infrastructure 2023 Database Administrator Professional:** This certification validates your skills in administering Oracle Database on OCI.

- Oracle Cloud Infrastructure 2023 Developer Associate:** This certification validates your skills in developing applications on OCI.

By earning OCI certifications, you can demonstrate your expertise and increase your value to organizations.

APPENDIX B: GLOSSARY OF CLOUD TERMS

CORE CLOUD COMPUTING TERMS

- Cloud Computing: The delivery of computing services, including servers, storage, databases, networking, software, analytics, and intelligence, over the Internet.

- Infrastructure as a Service (IaaS): A cloud service model that provides computing, storage, and networking resources.

- Platform as a Service (PaaS): A cloud service model that provides a platform for developing, deploying, and managing applications.

- Software as a Service (SaaS): A cloud service model that delivers software applications over the Internet.

- Public Cloud: A cloud computing environment that is available to the general public.

- Private Cloud: A cloud computing environment dedicated to a single organization.

- Hybrid Cloud: A cloud computing environment that combines public and private clouds.

- Multi-Cloud: A strategy that involves using multiple cloud providers.

OCI-SPECIFIC TERMS

- OCI: Oracle Cloud Infrastructure, a comprehensive cloud platform offered by Oracle.

- VNC: Virtual Network Compute, a network virtualization technology used in OCI.

- OCI Console: A web-based console for managing OCI resources.

- OCI CLI: The command-line interface for interacting with OCI.

- Autonomous Database: A fully automated, self-driving database service.

- Data Warehouse Cloud: A cloud-based data warehouse service for data analysis and business intelligence.

- Analytics Cloud: A cloud-based analytics platform for data visualization and predictive analytics.

- Function as a Service (FaaS): A serverless computing model that allows you to build and deploy applications without managing servers.

- Container Engine for Kubernetes (OKE): A managed Kubernetes service for deploying and managing containerized applications.

- Integration Cloud: A cloud-based integration platform for connecting applications and data.

- API Platform Cloud: A platform for designing, building, and managing APIs.

GENERAL IT TERMS

- Virtualization: The process of creating virtual instances of computing resources.

- Containerization: The packaging of software and its dependencies into a standardized unit.

- DevOps: A set of practices that combines software development and IT operations.

- CI/CD: Continuous Integration and Continuous Delivery, a methodology for software development.

- Infrastructure as Code (IaC): Managing infrastructure through code.

www.ingramcontent.com/pod-product-compliance
Lightning Source LLC
Chambersburg PA
CBHW071110240526
45469CB00006BD/2417